A 3-minute forever book

EAT
YOUR
PEAS™

for Mothers

By Cheryl Karpen
Gently Spoken Communications

Mother:
the most
beautiful word
on the lips of mankind.

Kahlil Gibran

10/25/04.

Dear Mother,

How do I begin to express gratitude to one who has given so unconditionally and asked for so little in return?

May this little book help me express what is on my mind and in my heart.

With all my love,

David

P.S. Happy Birthday! I Love You!

At
the heart
of this little book
is a
promise.
It's a promise from me to you
and
it goes like this:

If you ever need someone
to talk to
(to cry or brag to),
someone to listen
to what's in your heart
and on your mind,
I will be there for you.

I promise to listen
(really listen).

I promise to make an oasis
of time just for the two of us.

I promise to cherish your
memories
and
champion your dreams.

In the meantime,
there are some things I'd like you to know:

like how important you are to me,
how much I appreciate you,
and
how much I love and adore you.

Go ahead and turn the pages...

(Read often enough to commit to memory!)

You:
tender,
loving,
smart,
beautiful,
forgiving,
strong,
patient,
and
kind.

Me:
lucky

Many
of my
personal dreams
have
been
realized
because
of
how you loved me
and
what I learned
from you.

You make being a mom look easy.

I know it isn't.

You have no idea
how much you taught me
when I was trying so hard
not to learn!

For all those
aggravating
years
I thought the
world revolved around
me . . .

I'm sorry.
♡

I think of all the times
you must have been exhausted
and ready to give up,
but you didn't.

May I be as strong of heart
for those I love.

Remember all the times
I took you for granted?

I never want you to feel that way
ever again.

You are so very precious to me.

Although I will never know
your worry or heartache,
thank you for all the times
you let me
walk my own path
and
learn in my own way.

Kids have a knack
for saying things that are hurtful
(and I was no exception).

I hope it's not too late
to take back all those things
I said that were disrespectful.

I
never,
ever
want to
intentionally
hurt you.

I know there must have been
times when you felt
like **running away** in spirit.
Or for real.
Maybe you even did.

Thanks for always coming back to me.

I couldn't have grown up without
you!

bumps

scrapes

bruises

Thank you
for all the tears you wiped away,
for kisses that made it better,
and your smile that said it was safe
to face the world again.

blisters

heart hurts
♡♡

scuffles

I remember how you assured me everything would be okay — even when it felt like it was the end of my world. And you were right.

How did you become so wise?
(Why did it take me so long to notice?)

So much of who I am today is because of you.

You have guided me,
nurtured me,
and loved me.

I am grateful.

You
are more than
a remarkable mom.

You are a
remarkable woman.

I wish you
time for yourself:

a cozy corner,

a good book,

a soak in the tub...

You know those dreams you delayed
  so the rest of us could pursue ours?
Now it's my turn to cheer you on!

Go for it

Dream
  in
    color

Live
large

Take a chance

You can do it!

I believe in you.

After all these years of
magnificent mothering,
let me be the one to nudge you
to do something for yourself!

Have an adventure.
Travel light.
Help yourself to seconds.
Stay out late.
Dance in the rain.
Sleep in.
Ask for what you want.
Nap in the sun.
Accept compliments.
Be silly.

Celebrate yourself...
(You deserve it!)

Embrace
your
gifts...
(You have so very many!)

Indulge yourself...
(No one deserves it more!)

And most of all, stay healthy...

Remember to always...

Eat your peas!

Why Peas?

She was a vibrant, dazzling young woman with a promising future.
Yet, at sixteen, her world felt sad and hopeless.

I was living over 1800 miles away and wanted to let this very special young person in my life know I would be there for her across the miles and through the darkness. I wanted her to know she could call me any time, at any hour, and I would be there for her. And I wanted to give her a piece of my heart she could take with her anywhere—a reminder she was loved.
Really loved.

Her name is Maddy and she was the inspiration for my first PEAS book, Eat Your Peas for Young Adults. At the very beginning of her book I made a place to write in my phone number so she knew I was serious about being available. And right beside the phone number I put my promise to listen—really listen—whenever that call came.

Soon after the book was published, people began to ask me if I had the same promise and affirmation for adults. I realized it isn't just young people who need to be reminded how truly special they are. We all do.

Today Maddy is thriving and giving hope to others in her life.
If someone has given you this book it means you are a pretty amazing person to them and they wanted to let you know. Take it to heart.

Believe it, and remind yourself often.

Wishing you peas and plenty of joy,

Cheryl Karpen

S. If you are wondering why I named the collection, Eat Your Peas...it's my way of saying, "Stay healthy. I love and cherish you. I want you to live **forever**!"

With gratitude...

To my mother, Julia C. Karpen,
for being a phenomenal mother,
role model, and friend.
I wrote this book for you.

To my dear friend and illustrator, Sandy Fougner,
who is an absolute joy to collaborate with.
Her ability to make words
come alive through artful lettering and illustration is a
blessing to all who are graced by her work.

To editor, Suzanne Foust,
who is a gifted wordsmith
and PEAS treasured editor.

Other magnificent peas in the pod:
A special thank you to:
Gina Little, Emily Dhein,
Lana Siewert-Olson, Jairaj and Candace Abuvala,
and to my mentor, Tom Hill for
believing in me and the power of **Peas**.

About the author

In addition to her "passion for PEAS",
Cheryl is the owner of two gift and decorative accessory shop
located in the historic river town of Anoka, Minnesota:
Something Different and Pure Bliss.

An effervescent speaker, Cheryl
brings inspiration, insight and humor to corporations,
church groups and to other professional and community organizati

Find out more about her at www.SomethingDifferentSisters.cor

About the illustrator

Sandy Fougner artfully weaves a love
for design, illustration and interiors with being a
wife and mother of three sons.

Other books by Cheryl Karpen

The Eat Your Peas™ Collection

kes only 3-minutes to read but you'll want to hold on to it forever!

Eat Your Peas™ for Daughters
Eat Your Peas™ for Sisters
Eat Your Peas™ for Girlfriends
Eat Your Peas™ for Gardeners
Eat Your Peas™ for Young Adults

New titles are SPROUTING up all the time!

Hope and Encouragement Collection

To Let You Know I Care
Hope for a Hurting Heart
Can We Try Again? Finding a way to love

Eat Your Peas™ for Mothers

Copyright 2004, Cheryl Karpen

For more information or to locate a store near you contact

Gently Spoken Communications
P.O. Box 245
Anoka, Minnesota 55303
1-877-224-7886
www.gentlyspoken.com